To :

_____

The LORD himself goes before you
and will be with you; he will never
leave you nor forsake you.

DEUTERONOMY 31:8

FROM :

_____

Praying for Those We Love As They Serve Our Country
Copyright © 2003 by The Zondervan Corporation
ISBN 0-310-80577-5

Requests for information should be addressed to:
Inspirio, The gift group of Zondervan
Grand Rapids, Michigan 49530
http://www.inspiriogifts.com

Compiler: Doris Rikkers
Editor: Janice Jacobson - *My work on this project is dedicated to my
son, Petty Officer Third Class Carl Jacobson, serving aboard
the USS Kitty Hawk (CV 63).*
Design Manager: Amy J. Wenger
Design: UDG | DesignWorks, Sisters, Oregon

Printed in /PC/ 4 3 2 1

PRAYING *for* THOSE WE LOVE *as they serve* OUR COUNTRY

inspirio™

TABLE OF CONTENTS

Assurance....................7

Anxiety....................13

Blessings....................17

Comfort....................23

Confidence................29

Contentment............35

Courage....................39

Encouragement.........45

Faith........................49

Faithfulness..............55

Forgiveness................61

Future......................65

God's Love................71

God's Will................77

Grace........................83

Heaven....................89

Hope........................95

Integrity................101

Joy..........................107

Loneliness..............113

Patience..................119

Peace......................125

Praise......................131

Prayer....................135

Presence of God.......141

Protection..............147

Strength..................151

Stress......................157

Trust......................161

Wisdom..................165

ASSURANCE

*I have
summoned you by name;
you are mine.*

ISAIAH 43:1

The LORD is my shepherd, I shall not be in want.
   He makes me lie down in green pastures,
he leads me beside quiet waters.
   he restores my soul.
He guides me in paths of righteousness
   for his name's sake.
Even though I walk
   through the valley of the shadow of death,
I will fear no evil,
   for you are with me;
your rod and your staff,
   they comfort me.
You prepare a table before me
   in the presence of my enemies.
You anoint my head with oil;
   my cup overflows.
Surely goodness and love will follow me
   all the days of my life
and I will dwell in the house of the LORD
   forever.

PSALM 23

For I am convinced that neither death nor life, neither angels nor demons, neither the present nor the future, nor any powers, neither height nor depth, nor anything else in all creation, will be able to separate us from the love of God that is in Christ Jesus our Lord.

ROMANS 8:38–39

Though I walk in the midst of trouble,
*   you preserve my life;*
you stretch out your hand against the anger of my foes,
*   with your right hand you save me.*
The LORD will fulfill his purpose for me;
*   your love, O LORD, endures forever—*
*   do not abandon the works of your hands.*

PSALM 138:7–8

He will wipe every tear from their eyes. There will be no more death or mourning or crying or pain, for the old order of things has passed away. He who was seated on the throne said, "I am making everything new!" Then he said, "Write this down, for these words are trustworthy and true."

REVELATION 21:4–5

I sought the LORD, and he answered me;
    he delivered me from all my fears.

PSALM 34:4

For you have been born again, not of perishable seed, but of imperishable, through the living and enduring word of God. For,

> *"All men are like grass, and all their glory is like the flowers of the field; the grass withers and the flowers fall, but the word of the Lord stands forever."*

1 PETER 1:23–25

Jesus said to me, "My grace is sufficient for you, for my power is made perfect in weakness." Therefore I will boast all the more gladly about my weaknesses, so that Christ's power may rest on me. That is why, for Christ's sake, I delight in weaknesses, in insults, in hardships, in persecutions, in difficulties. For when I am weak, then I am strong.

2 CORINTHIANS 12:9–10

"Though the mountains be shaken
    and the hills be removed,
yet my unfailing love for you will not be shaken
    nor my covenant of peace be removed,"
    says the Lord, who has compassion on you.

ISAIAH 54:10

The LORD is my light and my salvation—
    whom shall I fear?
The LORD is the stronghold of my life—
    of whom shall I be afraid?
When evil men advance against me
    to devour my flesh,
when my enemies and my foes attack me,
    they will stumble and fall.
Though an army besiege me,
    my heart will not fear;
though war break out against me.
    even then will I be confident.

PSALM 27:1-3

The LORD is the strength of his people,
    a fortress of salvation for his anointed one.

PSALM 28:8

In God, whose word I praise,
in the LORD, whose word I praise—
in God I trust; I will not be afraid.
what can man do to me?
I am under vows to you, O God;
I will present my thank offerings to you.
For you have delivered me from death
and my feet from stumbling,
that I may walk before God
in the light of life.

PSALM 56:10–13

I am serene because
I know thou lovest me.
Because thou lovest me,
naught can move me from my peace.
Because thou lovest me,
I am as one to whom all good has come.

GAELIC

ANXIETY

*Cast all your anxiety
on God because he cares for you.*

1 PETER 5:7

O God,
My life is full of fears.
My days are consumed by anxious thoughts,
my nights by restless sleep.
Send me your peace, O God,
a peace that only you can give.
Release me of my overwhelming
anxiety and concerns.
Settle my anxious heart.
Calm my thoughts so that I can rest
in your love that knows no end,
in the knowledge that all events are in
your control,
and in your assurance that all will be well.
Amen.

DORIS W. RIKKERS

"Be still, and know that I am God;
　　I will be exalted among the nations,
　　I will be exalted in the earth."
PSALM 46:10

The LORD gives strength to his people;
　　the LORD blesses his people with peace.

PSALM 29:11

Jesus said, "Do not worry about tomorrow, for
tomorrow will worry about itself."

MATTHEW 6:34

We say with confidence,
　　"The Lord is my helper; I will not be afraid."

HEBREWS 13:6

Cast your cares on the LORD
　　and he will sustain you;
　　he will never let the righteous fall.

PSALM 55:22

Commit to the LORD whatever you do,
　　and your plans will succeed.

PROVERBS 16:3

Do not be anxious about anything, but in everything, by prayer and petition, with thanksgiving, present your requests to God. And the peace of God, which transcends all understanding, will guard your hearts and your minds in Christ Jesus.

PHILIPPIANS 4:6–7

Jesus said, "Look at the birds of the air; they do not sow or reap or store away in barns, and yet your heavenly Father feeds them. Are you not much more valuable than they?"

MATTHEW 6:26

When I said, "My foot is slipping,"
   your love, O LORD, supported me.
When anxiety was great within me,
   your consolation brought joy to my soul.

PSALM 94:18–19

BLESSINGS

*Blessed are
the people of whom this is true;
blessed are the people whose
God is the LORD.*

PSALM 144:15

The blessings of the Lord
rest and remain upon all his people,
in every land,
of every tongue;
the Lord meet in mercy all that seek him;
the Lord comfort all who suffer and mourn;
the Lord hasten his coming, and give us, his
people, the blessing of peace.

BISHOP HANDLEY MOULE

Blessed is the man who fears the LORD,
    who finds great delight in his commands.

PSALM 112:1

Taste and see that the LORD is good;
    blessed is the man who takes refuge in him.

PSALM 34:8

Blessed are those who have learned to acclaim you,
    who walk in the light of your presence, O LORD.

PSALM 89:15

The Lord blesses the home of the righteous.

PROVERBS 3:33

From the fullness of Christ's grace we have all
received one blessing after another.

JOHN 1:16

The Lord longs to be gracious to you;
    he rises to show you compassion.
For the Lord is a God of justice.
    Blessed are all who wait for him!

ISAIAH 30:18

Blessed are the poor in spirit,
    for theirs is the kingdom of heaven.
Blessed are those who mourn,
    for they will be comforted.
Blessed are the meek,
    for they will inherit the earth.
Blessed are those who hunger and thirst
        for righteousness,
    for they will be filled.
Blessed are the merciful,
    for they will be shown mercy.
Blessed are the pure in heart,
    for they will see God.
Blessed are the peacemakers,
    for they will be called sons of God.

MATTHEW 5:3–9

Surely, O LORD, you bless the righteous;
*   you surround them with your favor*
*   as with a shield.*

PSALM 5:12

The Lord bless you and keep you;
the Lord make his face shine upon you
*   and be gracious to you;*
the Lord turn his face toward you
*   and give you peace.*

NUMBERS 6:24–26

Every good and perfect gift is from above,
coming down from the Father of the heavenly
lights, who does not change like shifting shadows.

JAMES 1:17

The Lord richly blesses all who call on him.

ROMANS 10:12

"I will bless them and the places surrounding my
hill. I will send down showers in season; there
will be showers of blessing," declares the
Sovereign LORD.

EZEKIEL 34:26

Almighty Lord,
if we offer you a devoted mind and heart,
you will offer to us every blessing on earth
and in heaven.

You grant our deepest wishes.
You give food to the body and peace to the soul.
You look upon us with the love of
a mother for her children.

You created this beautiful earth all around us.
And in every plant and animal,
every tree and bird, your spirit dwells.

You have revealed yourself to me,
infusing my soul with the knowledge that you
are the source of all blessing.

And so I sing your praises day and night.
I who am feeble glorify you who are powerful.
I who am nothing devote myself
to you who are everything.

Atharva Veda

COMFORT

Be at rest once more,

O my soul,

for the LORD has been good to you.

PSALM 116:7

Jesus Christ is my comfort.
It is you who created us all.
There is only you, one God,
Father, Son, and Holy Spirit,
To whom homage and praise are due.

JANUARIUS OF CORDOVA

O LORD, you have searched me
and you know me.
You know when I sit and when I rise;
you perceive my thoughts from afar.
You discern my going out and my lying down;
you are familiar with all my ways.

PSALM 139:1–3

Let us acknowledge the Lord;
let us press on to acknowledge him.
As surely as the sun rises,
he will appear;
he will come to us like the winter rains,
like the spring rains that water the earth.

HOSEA 6:3

You gave me life and showed me kindness,
and in your providence watched over my
spirit, O God.

JOB 10:12

You are the God who sees me.

GENESIS 16:13

Praise be to the God and Father of our Lord Jesus
Christ, the Father of compassion and the God of
all comfort, who comforts us in all our troubles,
so that we can comfort those in any trouble with
the comfort we ourselves have received from God.

2 CORINTHIANS 1:3–4

The LORD is near to all who call on him.
to all who call on him in truth.

PSALM 145:18

"I will turn their mourning into gladness;
I will give them comfort and joy
instead of sorrow,"

declares the LORD.
JEREMIAH 31:13

Have faith in the LORD your God and
you will be upheld.

2 CHRONICLES 20:20

You, O LORD, have helped me and comforted me.

PSALM 86:17

Let the beloved of the LORD rest secure in him,
    for he shields him all day long,
    and the one the LORD loves rests
        between his shoulders.

DEUTERONOMY 33:12

May your unfailing love be my comfort, O LORD,
    according to your promise to your servant.

PSALM 119:76

"As a mother comforts her child,
    so will I comfort you;
    and you will be comforted," says the Lord.

ISAIAH 66:13

The LORD is good to all;
    he has compassion on all he has made.

PSALM 145:9

You understand, O LORD;
    remember me and care for me.

JEREMIAH 15:15

Lord Jesus Christ,
You are the gentle moon and joyful stars that
watch over the darkest night.
You are the source of all peace,
reconciling the whole universe to the Father.
You are the source of all rest,
calming troubled hearts,
and bringing sleep to weary bodies.
You are the sweetness that fills our minds
with quiet joy,
and can turn the worst nightmares into
dreams of heaven.
May I dream of your sweetness,
rest in your arms, be at one with your Father,
and be comforted in the knowledge that
you always watch over me.

Erasmus

CONFIDENCE

Blessed is
the man who trusts in the LORD,
whose confidence is in him.

JEREMIAH 17:7

The LORD is my rock, my fortress and
        my deliverer;
    my God is my rock, in whom I take refuge,
    my shield and the horn of my salvation.
He is my stronghold, my refuge and my savior—
    from violent men you save me.
I call to the LORD, who is worthy of praise,
    and I am saved from my enemies.
The waves of death swirled about me;
    the torrents of destruction overwhelmed me.
The cords of the grave coiled around me;
    the snares of death confronted me.
In my distress I called to the LORD;
    I called out to my God.
From his temple he heard my voice;
    my cry came to his ears.

2 SAMUEL 22:2–7

You, O LORD, have delivered my soul from death,
my eyes from tears,
my feet from stumbling,
that I may walk before the LORD
in the land of the living.

PSALM 116:8—9

I will be glad and rejoice in your love, O LORD,
for you saw my affliction
and knew the anguish of my soul.
You have not handed me over to the enemy
but have set my feet in a spacious place.

PSALM 31:7—8

If you make the Most High your dwelling—
even the LORD, who is my refuge—
then no harm will befall you,
no disaster will come near your tent.
For he will command his angels concerning you
to guard you in all your ways;
they will lift you up in their hands,
so that you will not strike your foot
against a stone.

PSALM 91:9—12

The LORD will be your confidence
and will keep your foot from being snared.

PROVERBS 3:26

I know that my Redeemer lives,
*   and that in the end he will stand*
*   upon the earth.*
I myself will see him
*   with my own eyes—I, and not another.*
*   How my heart yearns within me!*

JOB 19:25, 27

Such confidence as this is ours through Christ
before God. Not that we are competent in
ourselves to claim anything for ourselves, but our
competence comes from God.

2 CORINTHIANS 3:4-5

God did not give us a spirit of timidity, but a
spirit of power, of love and of self-discipline.

2 TIMOTHY 1:7

I am still confident of this:
*   I will see the goodness of the LORD*
*   in the land of the living.*

PSALM 27:13

Do you not know?
    Have you not heard?
The Lord is the everlasting God,
    the Creator of the ends of the earth.
He will not grow tired or weary,
    and his understanding no one can fathom.
He gives strength to the weary
    and increases the power of the weak.
Even youths grow tired and weary,
    and young men stumble and fall;
but those who hope in the Lord
    will renew their strength.
They will soar on wings like eagles;
    they will run and not grow weary,
    they will walk and not be faint.

ISAIAH 40:28–31

In Christ and through faith in him we may
approach God with freedom and confidence.

EPHESIANS 3:12

God has said,
"Never will I leave you;
    never will I forsake you."
So we say with confidence,
"The Lord is my helper; I will not be afraid.
    What can man do to me?"

HEBREWS 13:5–6

Do not throw away your confidence; it will be
richly rewarded.

HEBREWS 10:35

Our confidence
in Christ does not make us lazy,
negligent, or careless,
but on the contrary it awakens us,
urges us on,
and makes us active in living righteous lives
and doing good.
There is no self-confidence to
compare with this.

ULRICH ZWINGLI

CONTENTMENT

The fear of the LORD leads to life;

then one rests content,

untouched by trouble.

PROVERBS 19:23

Praise the LORD, O my soul,
    and forget not all his benefits—
who forgives all your sins
    and heals all your diseases,
who redeems your life from the pit
    and crowns you with love and compassion,
who satisfies your desires with good things
    so that your youth is renewed like the eagle's.

PSALM 103:2−5

Two things I ask of you, O LORD
    give me neither poverty nor riches,
    but give me only my daily bread.

PROVERBS 30:7−8

A man can do nothing better than to eat and
drink and find satisfaction in his work. This too,
I see, is from the hand of God, for without him,
who can eat or find enjoyment? To the man who
pleases him, God gives wisdom, knowledge and
happiness.

ECCLESIASTES 2:24−26

I said to the LORD, "You are my Lord;
    apart from you I have no good thing."

PSALM 16:2

I have learned to be content whatever the circumstances. I know what it is to be in need, and I know what it is to have plenty. I have learned the secret of being content in any and every situation, whether well fed or hungry, whether living in plenty or in want. I can do everything through him who gives me strength.

PHILIPPIANS 4:11–13

Godliness with contentment is great gain. For we brought nothing into the world, and we can take nothing out of it. But if we have food and clothing, we will be content with that. People who want to get rich fall into temptation and a trap and into many foolish and harmful desires that plunge men into ruin and destruction. For the love of money is a root of all kinds of evil. Some people, eager for money, have wandered from the faith and pierced themselves with many griefs.

1 TIMOTHY 6:6–10

The cheerful heart has a continual feast.

PROVERBS 15:15

Jesus said, "Do not store up for yourselves treasures on earth, where moth and rust destroy, and where thieves break in and steal. But store up for yourselves treasures in heaven, where moth and rust do not destroy, and where thieves do not break in and steal. For where your treasure is, there your heart will be also."

MATTHEW 6:19–21

O Almighty God,
Father and Lord of all the creatures,
by secret and indiscernible ways bringing good out
of evil:
give me wisdom from above;
teach me to be content in all changes of
person and condition,
to be temperate in prosperity,
and in adversity to be meek, patient,
and resigned;
and to look through the cloud,
in the meantime doing my duty with an
unwearied diligence,
and an undisturbed resolution.

JEREMY TAYLOR

COURAGE

Be strong and courageous.
Do not be terrified;
do not be discouraged,
for the LORD your God will be with you
wherever you go.

JOSHUA 1:9

I love you, O LORD, my strength.
The LORD is my rock, my fortress and my deliverer;
my God is my rock, in whom I take refuge. He is
my shield and the horn of my salvation,
my stronghold.
I call to the LORD, who is worthy of praise,
and I am saved from my enemies.

PSALM 18:1–3

Christ is faithful as a son over God's house. And
we are his house, if we hold on to our courage
and the hope of which we boast.

HEBREWS 3:6

Be strong and courageous, and do the work. Do
not be afraid or discouraged, for the LORD God,
my God, is with you. He will not fail you or
forsake you.

1 CHRONICLES 28:20

Though I have fallen, I will rise.
Though I sit in darkness,
the LORD will be my light.

MICAH 7:8

Be on your guard; stand firm in the faith;
be men of courage; be strong.

1 CORINTHIANS 16:13

Wait for the LORD;
be strong and take heart
and wait for the Lord.

PSALM 27:14

When you pass through the waters,
I will be with you;
and when you pass through the rivers,
they will not sweep over you.
When you walk through the fire,
you will not be burned;
the flames will not set you ablaze.
For I am the LORD, your God,
the Holy One of Israel, your Savior; . . .
you are precious and honored in my sight.

ISAIAH 43:2–4

Be strong and courageous. Do not be afraid or
terrified because of them, for the LORD your
God goes with you; he will never leave you nor
forsake you.

DEUTERONOMY 31:6

Act with courage, and may the LORD be with those who do well.

2 CHRONICLES 19:11

Jesus said to [the disciples]: "Take courage! It is I. Don't be afraid."

MATTHEW 14:27

Strengthen the feeble hands,
      steady the knees that give way;
say to those with fearful hearts,
      "Be strong, do not fear;
your God will come,
      he will come with vengeance."

ISAIAH 35:3–4

Be strong and take heart,
        all you who hope in the LORD.

PSALM 31:24

Jesus said, "Do not let your hearts be troubled. Trust in God; trust also in me."

JOHN 14:1

"No one will be able to stand up against you all the days of your life. As I was with Moses, so I will be with you; I will never leave you nor forsake you," says the LORD.

JOSHUA 1:5

I can do everything through him who gives me strength.

PHILIPPIANS 4:13

Be strong in the Lord and in his mighty power.

EPHESIANS 6:10

Be strong, show yourself a man, and observe what the LORD your God requires: Walk in his ways, and keep his decrees and commands.

1 KINGS 2:2−3

The eyes of the LORD range throughout the earth to strengthen those whose hearts are fully committed to him.

2 CHRONICLES 16:9

It is God who arms me with strength
    and makes my way perfect.

PSALM 18:32

For the Lord loves the just
 and will not forsake his faithful ones.
    They will be protected forever.

PSALM 37:28

You, O LORD, keep my lamp burning;
    my God turns my darkness into light.
With your help I can advance against a troop;
    with my God I can scale a wall.

PSALM 18:28–29

"I will strengthen them in the LORD
    and in his name they will walk,"
        declares the Lord.

ZECHARIAH 10:12

ENCOURAGEMENT

*May our Lord Jesus Christ himself
and God our Father,
who loved us and by his grace gave us
eternal encouragement and good hope,
encourage your hearts and strengthen you
in every good deed and word.*

2 THESSALONIANS 2:16–17

I lift up my eyes to the hills—
    where does my help come from?
My help comes from the LORD,
    the Maker of heaven and earth.
He will not let your foot slip—
    he who watches over you will not slumber;
indeed, he who watches over Israel
    will neither slumber nor sleep.
The LORD watches over you—
    the LORD is your shade at your right hand;
the sun will not harm you by day,
    nor the moon by night.
The LORD will keep you from all harm—
    he will watch over your life;
the LORD will watch over your coming and going
    both now and forevermore.

PSALM 121

"My mouth would encourage you;
comfort from my lips would bring you
relief," says the LORD.

JOB 16:5

May the LORD answer you when you are in distress;
may the name of the God of Jacob protect you.
May he send you help from the sanctuary
and grant you support from Zion.
May he give you the desire of your heart
and make all your plans succeed.
We will shout for joy when you are victorious
and will lift up our banners in the name
of our God.
May the LORD grant all your requests.

PSALM 20: 1–2, 4–5

The LORD said, "My Presence will go with you,
and I will give you rest."

EXODUS 33:14

The LORD is faithful to all his promises
and loving toward all he has made.
The LORD upholds all those who fall
and lifts up all who are bowed down.

PSALM 145:13–14

Praise be to the Lord, to God our Savior,
    who daily bears our burdens.

PSALM 68:19

Surely God is my help;
    the Lord is the one who sustains me.

PSALM 54:4

You hear, O LORD, the desire of the afflicted;
    you encourage them, and you listen to their cry.

PSALM 10:17

We do not lose heart. Though outwardly we
are wasting away, yet inwardly we are being
renewed day by day.

2 CORINTHIANS 4:16

He will cover you with his feathers,
    and under his wings you will find refuge;
    his faithfulness will be your shield
        and rampart.

PSALM 91:4

FAITH

We live by faith, not by sight.

2 CORINTHIANS 5:7

Lord,
By faith I know you live and reign
over all creation.
By faith I know you love me, watch over me,
and everyone I love,
hour-by-hour, day-by-day.
By faith I know you are
a loving and merciful God who saves me
through your son Jesus Christ.
Increase my faith, O God.
Make me strong and courageous when
my faith is challenged so that I may
always boldly declare:
You are my God.
Amen

DORIS W. RIKKERS

Jesus told [Thomas], "Because you have seen me,
you have believed; blessed are those who have not
seen and yet have believed."

JOHN 20:29

Faith is being sure of what we hope for and
certain of what we do not see.

HEBREWS 11:1

Without faith it is impossible to please God,
because anyone who comes to him must believe
that he exists and that he rewards those who
earnestly seek him.

HEBREWS 11:6

God redeemed us ... so that by faith we might
receive the promise of the Spirit.

GALATIANS 3:14

I pray that out of his glorious riches he may
strengthen you with power through his Spirit in
your inner being, so that Christ may dwell in your
hearts through faith.

EPHESIANS 3:16–17

A faithful man will be richly blessed.

PROVERBS 28:20

Everyone born of God overcomes the world.
This is the victory that has overcome the world,
even our faith.

1 JOHN 5:4

Since we have been justified through faith,
we have peace with God through our Lord
Jesus Christ.

ROMANS 5:1

To all who received him, to those who believed
in his name, he gave the right to become children
of God—children born not of natural descent,
nor of human decision or a husband's will,
but born of God.

JOHN 1:12–13

Jesus said, "Everything is possible for
him who believes."

MARK 9:23

Faith comes from hearing the message, and the message is heard through the word of Christ.

ROMANS 10:17

Jesus said, "I tell you the truth, if you have faith as small as a mustard seed, you can say to this mountain, 'Move from here to there' and it will move. Nothing will be impossible for you."

MATTHEW 17:20

Let us fix our eyes on Jesus, the author and perfecter of our faith, who for the joy set before him endured the cross, scorning its shame, and sat down at the right hand of the throne of God. Consider him who endured such opposition from sinful men, so that you will not grow weary and lose heart.

HEBREWS 12:2-3

It is by faith you stand firm.

2 CORINTHIANS 1:24

I have fought the good fight, I have finished the race, I have kept the faith.

2 TIMOTHY 4:7

Make very effort to add to your faith, goodness;
and to goodness, knowledge; and to knowledge
self-control; and to self-control, perseverance;
and to perseverance, godliness; and to godliness,
brotherly kindness; and to brotherly kindness,
love. For if you possess these qualities in
increasing measure, they will keep you from
being ineffective and unproductive in your
knowledge of our Lord Jesus Christ.

2 PETER 1:5-8

In the gospel a righteousness from God is
revealed, a righteousness that is by faith from first
to last, just as it is written: "The righteous will
live by faith."

ROMANS 1:17

My faith looks up to Thee,
Thou Lamb of Calvary, Savior divine;
Now hear me when I pray,
Take all my sin away,
O let me from this day be wholly Thine!

RAY PALMER

FAITHFULNESS

The Lord is faithful,
and he will strengthen and protect you
from the evil one.

2 THESSALONIANS 3:3

Lord, by your own hand you brought
to light the eternal fabric of the universe and
created the world of humankind.

From generation to generation you are faithful,
right in your judgments,
glorious in majesty and might.

Lord, show forth the light of your face
upon us in peace for our help;

Deliver us from those who hate us
without a cause;

To us and to all humankind
grant peace and concord,
even as you did to those who came before us when
they called upon you truthfully
and faithfully;

And cause us to be obedient
both to your own almighty and glorious name, and
to all who bear rule over us upon earth.

CLEMENT OF ROME

I will praise you, O Lord, among the nations;
I will sing of you among the peoples.
For great is your love, reaching to the heavens;
your faithfulness reaches to the skies.

PSALM 57: 9–10

Know therefore that the LORD your God is God;
he is the faithful God, keeping his covenant of
love to a thousand generations of those who love
him and keep his commands.

DEUTERONOMY 7:9

The LORD is good and his love endures forever;
his faithfulness continues through
all generations.

PSALM 100:5

O LORD, you are my God;
I will exalt you and praise your name,
for in perfect faithfulness
you have done marvelous things,
things planned long ago.

ISAIAH 25:1

Great is your love, O God, higher than the heavens;
your faithfulness reaches to the skies.

PSALM 108:4

Those who know your name will trust in you,
for you, LORD, have never forsaken
those who seek you.

PSALM 9:10

If we confess our sins, God is faithful and just
and will forgive us our sins and purify us from
all unrighteousness.

1 JOHN 1:9

Let us hold unswervingly to the hope we profess,
for he who promised is faithful.

HEBREWS 10:23

The LORD rewards every man for his
righteousness and faithfulness.

1 SAMUEL 26:23

The works of the LORD's hands are faithful and just;
all his precepts are trustworthy.
They are steadfast for ever and ever,
done in faithfulness and uprightness.

PSALM 111:7−8

To the faithful you show yourself faithful, LORD,
   to the blameless you show yourself blameless.

PSALM 18:25

"I will betroth you to me forever;
   I will betroth you in righteousness and
      justice,
   in love and compassion.
I will betroth you in faithfulness,
   and you will acknowledge the Lord,"
                        says the Lord.

HOSEA 2:19—20

Blessed is he whose help is the God of Jacob,
   whose hope is in the LORD his God,
the Maker of heaven and earth,
   the sea, and everything in them—
   the LORD, who remains faithful forever.

PSALM 146:5—6

May the LORD our God be with us as he was with our fathers; may he never leave us nor forsake us.

1 KINGS 8:57

Because of the Lord's great love
we are not consumed,
for his compassions never fail.
They are new every morning;
great is your faithfulness.

LAMENTATIONS 3:22—23

God sends his love and his faithfulness.

PSALM 57:3

The LORD came down in the cloud and stood there with Moses and proclaimed his name, the LORD. And he passed in front of Moses, proclaiming, "The LORD, the LORD, the compassionate and gracious God, slow to anger, abounding in love and faithfulness, maintaining love to thousands.

EXODUS 34:5-6

FORGIVENESS

Repent and be baptized, every one of you,
in the name of Jesus Christ for the
forgiveness of your sins.
And you will receive the gift of the Holy Spirit.
The promise is for you and your children
and for all who are far off—for all whom
the Lord our God will call.

ACTS 2:38–39

Who is a God like you,
   who pardons sin and forgives the transgression
   of the remnant of his inheritance?
You do not stay angry forever
   but delight to show mercy.

MICAH 7:18

Bless the LORD, O my soul;
   and forget not all his benefits—
who forgives all your sins
   and heals all your diseases.

PSALM 103:2–3

I want you to know that through Jesus the
forgiveness of sins is proclaimed to you.

ACTS 13:38

Jesus said, "When you stand praying, if you hold
anything against anyone, forgive him, so that your
Father in heaven may forgive you your sins."

MARK 11:25

Be kind and compassionate to one another,
forgiving each other, just as in Christ God
forgave you.

EPHESIANS 4:32

Seek the Lord while he may be found;
call on him while he is near.
Let the wicked forsake his way
and the evil man his thoughts.
Let him turn to the Lord, and he will
have mercy on him,
and to our God, for he will freely pardon.

ISAIAH 55:6–7

You are a forgiving God, gracious and
compassionate, slow to anger and abounding
in love.

NEHEMIAH 9:17

If my people, who are called by my name,
will humble themselves and pray and seek my
face and turn from their wicked ways, then will
I hear from heaven and will forgive their sin and
will heal their land.

2 CHRONICLES 7:14

If you, O LORD, kept a record of sins,
  O LORD, who could stand?
But with you there is forgiveness;
  therefore you are feared.

PSALM 130:3-4

Jesus said, "If you forgive men when they
sin against you, your heavenly Father will
also forgive you."

MATTHEW 6:14

Create in me a pure heart, O God,
  and renew a steadfast spirit within me.
Do not cast me from your presence
  or take your Holy Spirit from me.
Restore to me the joy of your salvation
  and grant me a willing spirit, to sustain me.

PSALM 51:10-12

FUTURE

*The plans of the
LORD stand firm forever,
the purposes of his heart through
all generations.*

<small>PSALM 33:11</small>

Our Father in heaven,
You are the only one who knows and sees all—
of our past, our present, our future.
Hold us securely in your love
as we face each tomorrow.
Guide us and protect us with your
mighty and powerful hand.
Reassure us that you and you alone are
the Controller of all that is yet to come,
in this world and the next.
Amen

DORIS W. RIKKERS

There is surely a future hope for you,
and your hope will not be cut off.

PROVERBS 23:18

"I know the plans I have for you," declares the LORD, "plans to prosper you and not to harm you, plans to give you hope and a future. Then you will call upon me and come and pray to me, and I will listen to you."

JEREMIAH 29:11–12

As it is written:
> "No eye has seen,
>> no ear has heard,
>
> no mind has conceived
>> what God has prepared for those
>>
>> who love him"—

but God has revealed it to us by his Spirit.

The Spirit searches all things, even the deep things of God.

1 CORINTHIANS 2:9–10

> "Forget the former things;
>> do not dwell on the past.
>
> See, I am doing a new thing!
>> Now it springs up; do you not perceive it?
>
> I am making a way in the desert
>> and streams in the wasteland,"

declares the LORD.

ISAIAH 43:18–19

Then I saw a new heaven and a new earth, for the first heaven and the first earth had passed away, and there was no longer any sea. I saw the Holy City, the new Jerusalem, coming down out of heaven from God, prepared as a bride beautifully dressed for her husband. And I heard a loud voice from the throne saying, "Now the dwelling of God is with men, and he will live with them. They will be his people, and God himself will be with them and be their God."

REVELATION 21:1–3

If you will look to God
    and plead with the Almighty,
if you are pure and upright,
    even now he will rouse himself on your
    behalf
    and restore you to your rightful place.
Your beginnings will seem humble,
    so prosperous will your future be.

JOB 8:5–7

Now we are children of God, and what we will be has not yet been made known. But we know that when Christ appears, we shall be like him, for we shall see him as he is.

1 JOHN 3:2

All the days ordained for me
were written in your book
before one of them came to be.

PSALM 139:16

"My Spirit, who is on you, and my words that
I have put in your mouth will not depart from
your mouth, or from the mouths of your
children, or from the mouths of their descendants
from this time on and forever," says the LORD.

ISAIAH 59:21

The Plans of the LORD stand firm forever,
the purpose of his heart through all
generations.

PSALM 33:11

Jesus said, "In the future you will see the Son of
Man sitting at the right hand of the Mighty One
and coming on the clouds of heaven."

MATTHEW 26:64

O Lord,
we beseech thee to deliver us
from the fear
of the unknown future;
from fear of failure;
from fear of poverty;
from fear of bereavement;
from fear of loneliness;
from fear of sickness and pain;
from fear of age;
and from fear of death.

Help us, O Father,
by thy grace to love and fear thee only,
fill our hearts with cheerful courage and loving
trust in thee;
through our Lord and Master Jesus Christ.

Akanu Ibaim, Nigeria

GOD'S LOVE

God, the Lord, will show compassion,
so great is his unfailing love.

LAMENTATIONS 3:32

Jesus,
how sweet is the very thought of you!
You fill my heart with joy.
The sweetness of your love surpasses the sweetness of
honey.
Nothing sweeter than you can be described;
no words can express the joy of your love.
Only those who have tasted your love for themselves
can comprehend it.

In your love you listen to all my prayers,
even when my wishes are childish,
my words confused, and my thoughts foolish.
And you answer my prayers,
not according to my own misdirected desires, which
would bring only bitter misery,
but according to my real needs,
which brings me sweet joy.

Thank you, Jesus, for giving yourself to me.

BERNARD OF CLAIRVAUX

The LORD your God is with you,
    he is mighty to save.
He will take great delight in you,
    he will quiet you with his love,
    he will rejoice over you with singing.

ZEPHANIAH 3:17

The LORD is gracious and compassionate,
    slow to anger and rich in love.

PSALM 145:8

Turn, O LORD, and deliver me;
    save me because of your unfailing love.

PSALM 6:4

Let them give thanks to the LORD for his unfailing love
    and his wonderful deeds for men,
for he satisfies the thirsty
    and fills the hungry with good things.

PSALM 107:8-9

God has poured out his love into our hearts by
the Holy Spirit, whom he has given us.

ROMANS 5:5

From everlasting to everlasting
    the LORD's love is with those who fear him,
    and his righteousness with their children's
    children.

PSALM 103:17

God demonstrates his own love for us in this:
While we were still sinners, Christ died for us.

ROMANS 5:8

Grace, mercy and peace from God the
Father and from Jesus Christ, the Father's Son,
will be with us in truth and love.

2 JOHN 1:3

May the grace of the Lord Jesus Christ, and the
love of God, and the fellowship of the Holy Spirit
be with you all.

2 CORINTHIANS 13:14

If anyone obeys his word, God's love is truly
made complete in him.

1 JOHN 2:5

"For God so loved the world that he gave his one
and only Son, that whoever believes in him shall
not perish but have eternal life."

JOHN 3:16

The LORD appeared to us in the past, saying:
> *"I have loved you with an everlasting love;*
> *I have drawn you with loving-kindness."*

JEREMIAH 31:3

I trust in you, O LORD;
> *I say, "You are my God."*
My times are in your hands;
> *deliver me from my enemies*
> *and from those who pursue me.*
Let you face shine on your servant;
> *save me in your unfailing love.*

PSALM 31:14–16

Jesus said, "The Father himself loves you because you have loved me and have believed that I came from God."

JOHN 16:27

Your love, O LORD, reaches to the heavens,
   your faithfulness to the skies.

PSALM 36:5

O God of love,
may the peace of the Lord Jesus Christ,
the love of the Father,
and the fellowship of the Holy Spirit
be with all of us.
Surround us with your loving arms
and shelter us with your peace,
now and forevermore.
Amen

DORIS W. RIKKERS

GOD'S WILL

In Christ we were also chosen,
having been predestined according to
the plan of him who works out everything
in conformity with the purpose of his will,
in order that we, who were the first
to hope in Christ, might be for the praise
of his glory.

EPHESIANS 1:11–12

I do not eat, Lord,
just because I am hungry,
nor merely to give me pleasure.
No, I eat because, in your providence, you have
created me with the need for food.

When I must turn to a friend for help,
I recognize that you have created man to help,
comfort and encourage each other.
And since this is your wish, I will turn to
those whose friendship is your gift to me.

When I have good reason
to be afraid of something,
I recognize that you want me to be afraid,
in order that I should take suitable steps to
avoid danger. So I shall act on my fear,
according to your will. If fear becomes excessive, I
can turn to you, knowing that as your child
I can nestle in your loving arms.

Thus, Lord, I try to do the right thing.
And when I have done all I can, I know that
whatever happens is an expression of your will.

FRANCIS OF SALES

Teach me to do your will,
    for you are my God,
may your good Spirit
    lead me on level ground.

PSALM 143:10

Do not conform any longer to the pattern of this world, but be transformed by the renewing of your mind. Then you will be able to test and approve what God's will is—his good, pleasing and perfect will.

ROMANS 12:2

It is God's will that you should be sanctified ... that each of you should learn to control his own body in a way that is holy and honorable.

1 THESSALONIANS 4:3–4

I desire to do your will, O my God,
    your law is within my heart.

PSALM 40:8

The world and its desires pass away, but the man
who does the will of God lives forever.

1 JOHN 2:17

Jesus said, "Whoever does the will of my Father in
heaven is my brother and sister and mother."

MATTHEW 12:50

You ought to say, "If it is the Lord's will, we will
live and do this or that."

JAMES 4:15

May the God of peace, who through the blood of
the eternal covenant brought back from the dead
our Lord Jesus, that great Shepherd of the sheep,
equip you with everything good for doing his
will, and may he work in us what is pleasing to
him, through Jesus Christ, to whom be glory for
ever and ever. Amen.

HEBREWS 13:20—21

Jesus declared, "I have come down from heaven
not to do my will but to do the will of him who
sent me. And this is the will of him who sent me,
that I shall lose none of all that he has given me,
but raise them up at the last day."

JOHN 6:38—39

Be joyful always; pray continually; give thanks
in all circumstances, for this is God's will for
you in Christ Jesus.

1 THESSALONIANS 5:16–18

He who searches our hearts knows the mind
of the Spirit, because the Spirit intercedes for the
saints in accordance with God's will.

ROMANS 8:27

Do not throw away your confidence; it will be
richly rewarded. You need to persevere so that
when you have done the will of God, you will
receive what he has promised.

HEBREWS 10:35–36

It is God who works in you to will and to act
according to his good purpose.

PHILIPPIANS 2:13

Stand firm in all the will of God,
mature and fully assured.

COLOSSIANS 4:12

In him we were also chosen, having been predestined according to the plan of him who works out everything in conformity with the purpose of his will, in order that we, who were the first to hope in Christ, might be for the praise of his glory.

EPHESIANS 1:11—12

Grace and peace to you from God our Father and the Lord Jesus Christ, who gave himself for our sins to rescue us from the present evil age, according to the will of our God and Father, to whom be glory for ever and ever. Amen.

GALATIANS 1:3—5

Almighty, eternal,
just and merciful God,
grant us the desire
to do only what pleases you,
and the strength to do only what you command.
Cleanse our souls, enlighten our minds,
and inflame our hearts with your Holy Spirit,
that we may follow in the footsteps of
your beloved Son, Jesus Christ.

ST. FRANCIS OF ASSISI

GRACE

*It is by grace you have
been saved.*

Ephesians 2:5

Lord God,
open my heart and pour into it the grace
of your Holy Spirit.
By this grace may I always seek
to do what is pleasing to you;
may my thoughts always reflect your thoughts; and
may my affections be solely directed
towards the unending joys of heaven.
Thus may I on earth fulfill your commandments,
that I may be worthy of your
everlasting reward.

BEDE

God raised us up with Christ and seated us with him in the heavenly realms in Christ Jesus, in order that in the coming ages he might show the incomparable riches of his grace, expressed in his kindness to us in Christ Jesus.

EPHESIANS 2:6–7

God is able to make all grace abound to you, so that in all things at all times, having all that you need, you will abound in every good work. As it is written:
"He has scattered abroad his gifts to the poor;
*   his righteousness endures forever."*

2 CORINTHIANS 9:8–9

For it is by grace you have been saved, through faith—and this not from yourselves, it is the gift of God—not by works, so that no one can boast.

EPHESIANS 2:8–9

We believe it is through the grace of our Lord Jesus that we are saved.

ACTS 15:11

All have sinned and fall short of the glory of God, and are justified freely by his grace through the redemption that came by Christ Jesus.

ROMANS 3:23–24

At the present time there is a remnant chosen by grace. And if by grace, then it is no longer by works; if it were, grace would no longer be grace.

ROMANS 11:5–6

The grace of God that brings salvation has appeared to all.

TITUS 2:11

God saved us, not because of righteous things we had done, but because of his mercy. He saved us through the washing of rebirth and renewal by the Holy Spirit, whom he poured out on us generously through Jesus Christ our Savior, so that, having been justified by his grace, we might become heirs having the hope of eternal life.

TITUS 3:5–7

And the child [Jesus] grew and became strong; he was filled with wisdom, and the grace of God was upon him.

LUKE 2:40

Now this is our boast: Our conscience testifies
that we have conducted ourselves in the world,
and especially in our relations with you,
in the holiness and sincerity that are from God.
We have done so not according to worldly
wisdom but according to God's grace.

2 CORINTHIANS 1:12

God opposes the proud,
    but gives grace to the humble.

1 PETER 5:5

You then, ... be strong in the grace
that is in Christ Jesus.

2 TIMOTHY 2:1

To each one of us grace has been given as Christ
apportioned it.

EPHESIANS 4:7

Let us then approach the throne of grace with
confidence, so that we may receive mercy and
find grace to help us in our time of need.

HEBREWS 4:16

Praise be to the God and Father of our Lord Jesus
Christ, who has blessed us in the heavenly realms
with every spiritual blessing in Christ.
For he chose us in him before the creation of
the world to be holy and blameless in his sight.
In love he predestined us to be adopted as his
sons through Jesus Christ, in accordance with his
pleasure and will—to the praise of his glorious
grace, which he has freely given us in the One he
loves. In him we have redemption through his
blood, the forgiveness of sins, in accordance with
the riches of God's grace that he lavished on us
with all wisdom and understanding.

EPHESIANS 1:3-8

The gracious hand of our God is on everyone
who looks to him.

EZRA 8:22

May God be gracious to us and bless us
and make his face shine upon us.

PSALM 67:1

HEAVEN

Jesus said,
"Rejoice and be glad, because great
is your reward in heaven."

MATTHEW 5:12

Bring us,
O Lord God, at our last awakening into
the house and gate of heaven,
to enter into that gate and dwell in that house,
where there shall be no darkness nor dazzling,
but one equal light;
no noise nor silence,
but one equal music;
no fears nor hopes,
but one equal possession;
no ends nor beginnings,
but one equal eternity;
in the habitations for your glory and dominion,
world without end.

JOHN DONNE

Jesus said, "In my Father's house are many rooms; if it were not so, I would have told you. I am going there to prepare a place for you. And if I go and prepare a place for you, I will come back and take you to be with me that you also may be where I am. You know the way to the place where I am going."

JOHN 14:2–4

We know that if the earthly tent we live in is destroyed, we have a building from God, an eternal house in heaven, not built by human hands.

2 CORINTHIANS 5:1

Our citizenship is in heaven. And we eagerly await a Savior from there, the Lord Jesus Christ.

PHILIPPIANS 3:20

In keeping with his promise we are looking forward to a new heaven and a new earth, the home of righteousness.

2 PETER 3:13

You alone are the LORD. You made the heavens, even the highest heavens, and all their starry host, the earth and all that is on it, the seas and all that is in them. You give life to everything, and the multitudes of heaven worship you.

NEHEMIAH 9:6

God raised us up with Christ and seated us with him in the heavenly realms in Christ Jesus, in order that in the coming ages he might show the incomparable riches of his grace, expressed in his kindness to us in Christ Jesus.

EPHESIANS 2:6–7

I looked and there before me was a great multitude that no one could count, from every nation, tribe, people and language, standing before the throne [in heaven] and in front of the Lamb. They were wearing white robes and were holding palm branches in their hands.

REVELATION 7:9

I consider that our present sufferings are not worth comparing with the glory that will be revealed in us.

ROMANS 8:18

The angel showed me the river of the water of life, as clear as crystal, flowing from the throne of God and of the Lamb down the middle of the great street of the city. On each side of the river stood the tree of life, bearing twelve crops of fruit, yielding its fruit every month.

And the leaves of the tree are for the healing of the nations. No longer will there be any curse. The throne of God and of the Lamb will be in the city, and his servants will serve him. They will see his face, and his name will be on their foreheads. There will be no more night. They will not need the light of a lamp or the light of the sun, for the Lord God will give them light.

And they will reign for ever and ever.

REVELATION 22:3–5

You guide me with your counsel,
and afterward you will take me into glory.
Whom have I in heaven but you?
And earth has nothing I desire besides you.

PSALM 73:24–25

Jesus said, "Rejoice that your names are written in heaven."

LUKE 10:20

The heavens declare the glory of God;
    the skies proclaim the work of his hands.

PSALM 19:1

Our light and momentary troubles are achieving
for us an eternal glory that far outweighs them all.

2 CORINTHIANS 4:17

Never again will they hunger;
    never again will they thirst.
The sun will not beat upon them,
    nor any scorching heat.
For the Lamb at the center of the throne
    will be their shepherd;
    he will lead them to springs of living water.
And God will wipe away every tear
        from their eyes.

REVELATION 7:16–17

HOPE

Those who hope in the LORD
will renew their strength.
They will soar on wings like eagles;
they will run and not grow weary,
they will walk and not be faint.

ISAIAH 40:31

The physician our Saviour
is all powerful.
He restores those who worship
the Lord and hope in him.
He heals not by men's cunning,
but by his word.
Though he dwells in heaven,
he is present everywhere.
All praise to him.

ANDRONICUS OF POMPEIOPOLIS

Praise be to the God and Father of our Lord Jesus Christ! In his great mercy, he has given us new birth into a living hope through the resurrection of Jesus Christ from the dead, and into an inheritance that can never perish, spoil or fade—kept in heaven for you.

1 PETER 1:3–4

We know that in all things God works for the good of those who love him, who have been called according to his purpose. What, then, shall we say in response to this? If God is for us, who can be against us?

ROMANS 8:28, 31

The Lord performs wonders that
      cannot be fathomed,
    miracles that cannot be counted.
He bestows rain on the earth;
    he sends water upon the countryside.
The lowly he sets on high,
    and those who mourn are lifted to safety.

JOB 5:9–11

The eyes of the LORD are on those who fear him,
    on those whose hope is in his unfailing love.

PSALM 33:18

I saw the Lord always before me.
    Because he is at my right hand,
    I will not be shaken.
Therefore my heart is glad and my tongue rejoices;
    my body also will live in hope.

ACTS 2:25–26

Hope that is seen is no hope at all. Who hopes for what he already has? But if we hope for what we do not yet have, we wait for it patiently.

ROMANS 8:24–25

"You will know that I am the Lord;
    those who hope in me will not be
        disappointed," says the Lord.

ISAIAH 49:23

We wait in hope for the LORD;
    he is our help and our shield.
In him our hearts rejoice,
    for we trust in his holy name.
May your unfailing love rest upon us, O LORD,
    even as we put our hope in you.

PSALM 33:20–22

Through Christ you believe in God, who raised him from the dead and glorified him, and so your faith and hope are in God.

1 PETER 1:21

I pray also that the eyes of your heart may be enlightened in order that you may know the hope to which he has called you, the riches of his glorious inheritance in the saints, and his incomparable great power for us who believe.

EPHESIANS 1:18–19

The LORD is good to those whose hope is in him,
    to the one who seeks him;
it is good to wait quietly
    for the salvation of the Lord.

LAMENTATIONS 3:25–26

I consider that our present sufferings are not worth comparing with the glory that will be revealed in us.

ROMANS 8:18

What was glorious has no glory now in comparison with the surpassing glory. And if what was fading away came with glory, how much greater is the glory of that which lasts! Therefore, since we have such a hope, we are very bold.

2 CORINTHIANS 3:10–12

Prepare your minds for action; be self-controlled;
set your hope fully on the grace to be given you
when Jesus Christ is revealed.

1 PETER 1:13

Why are you downcast, O my soul?
Why so disturbed within me?
Put your hope in God,
for I will yet praise him,
my Savior and my God.

PSALM 42:11

The LORD watches over you—
the LORD is your shade at your right hand;
the sun will not harm you by day,
nor the moon by night.
The LORD will keep you from all harm—
he will watch over your life;
the LORD will watch over your coming and
going
both now and forevermore.

PSALM 121:5–8

INTEGRITY

*May integrity
and uprightness protect me,
because my hope is in you,
O Lord.*

PSALM 25:21

Almighty God,
Father of our Lord Jesus Christ,
grant, we pray, that we might be grounded
and settled in your truth by the coming
of your Holy Spirit into our heart.
What we do not know,
reveal to us;
What is lacking within us,
make complete;
That which we do know,
confirm in us;
And keep us blameless in your service,
through Jesus Christ our Lord.

CLEMENT OF ROME

Search me, O God, and know my heart;
*   test me and know my anxious thoughts.*
See if there is any offensive way in me,
*   and lead me in the way everlasting.*

PSALM 139:23–24

I know, my God, that you test the heart and
are pleased with integrity.

1 CHRONICLES 29:17

Let us not become weary in doing good,
for at the proper time we will reap a harvest
if we do not give up.

GALATIANS 6:9

Jesus said, "Whoever can be trusted with very
little can also be trusted with much, and whoever
is dishonest with very little will also be dishonest
with much."

LUKE 16:10

In everything set them an example by doing what is good. In your teaching show integrity, seriousness and soundness of speech that cannot be condemned, so that those who oppose you may be ashamed because they have nothing bad to say about us.

TITUS 2:7–8

Let love and faithfulness never leave you;
bind them around your neck,
write them on the tablet of your heart.
Then you will win favor and a good name
in the sight of God and man.

PROVERBS 3:3–4

Give everyone what you owe him:
If you owe taxes, pay taxes; if revenue,
then revenue; if respect, then respect;
if honor, then honor. Let no debt remain
outstanding, except the continuing debt to
love one another, for he who loves his
fellowman has fulfilled the law.

ROMANS 13:7–8

I know that you are pleased with me, LORD,
for my enemy does not triumph over me.
In my integrity you uphold me
and set me in your presence forever.

PSALM 41:11−12

The man of integrity walks securely,
but he who takes crooked paths will be found out.

PROVERBS 10:9

LORD, who may dwell in your sanctuary?
Who may live on your holy hill?
He whose walk is blameless
and who does what is righteous,
who speaks the truth from his heart.

PSALM 15:1−2

We are taking pains to do what is right,
not only in the eyes of the Lord but also in
the eyes of men.

2 CORINTHIANS 8:21

Lord, make me an
instrument of your peace!
Where there is hatred,
let me sow love;
where there is injury, pardon;
where there is doubt, faith;
where there is darkness, light;
and where there is sadness, joy.

O divine Master,
grant that I may not
So much seek to be consoled
as to console;
to be understood
as to understand;
to be loved;
for it is in giving
that we receive;
it is in pardoning
that we are pardoned;
and it is in dying
that we are born to Eternal Life.

St. Francis of Asssisi

JOY

Though you have not seen him,
you love him;
and even though you do not see him now,
you believe in him and are filled with an
inexpressible and glorious joy.

1 PETER 1:8

As the hand is made for holding
and the eye for seeing,
thou hast fashioned me for joy.
Share with me the vision that shall find it
everywhere;
in the wild violet's beauty;
in the lark's melody;
in the face of a steadfast man;
in a child's smile
in a mother's love
in the purity of Jesus.

GAELIC PRAYER

Satisfy us in the morning with your unfailing love,
    O LORD,
that we may sing for joy and be glad all our days.

PSALM 90:14

Shout for joy to the LORD, all the earth.
    Worship the LORD with gladness;
    come before him with joyful songs.
Know that the LORD is God.
    It is he who made us, and we are his;
    we are his people, the sheep of his pasture.

PSALM 100:1—3

Do not grieve, for the joy of the LORD
is your strength.

NEHEMIAH 8:10

The LORD has done great things for us,
    and we are filled with joy.

PSALM 126:3

May the God of hope fill you with all joy
and peace as you trust in him, so that you may
overflow with hope by the power of the
Holy Spirit.

ROMANS 15:13

Rejoice in the Lord always. I will say it again: Rejoice! Let your gentleness be evident to all. The Lord is near. Do not be anxious about anything, but in everything, by prayer and petition, with thanksgiving, present your requests to God. And the peace of God, which transcends all understanding, will guard your hearts and your minds in Christ Jesus.

PHILIPPIANS 4:4–7

Sing joyfully to the LORD, you righteous;
it is fitting for the upright to praise him.

PSALM 33:1

You have made known to me the path of life;
you will fill me with joy in your presence,
with eternal pleasures at your right hand.

PSALM 16:11

Weeping may remain for a night,
but rejoicing comes in the morning.

PSALM 30:5

Those who sow in tears
    will reap with songs of joy.

PSALM 126:5

With joy you will draw water
    from the wells of salvation.

ISAIAH 12:3

The ransomed of the Lord will return.
They will enter Zion with singing;
    everlasting joy will crown their heads.
Gladness and joy will overtake them,
    and sorrow and sighing will flee away.

ISAIAH 35:10

Our mouths were filled with laughter,
    our tongues with songs of joy.
Then it was said among the nations,
    "The LORD has done great things for them."
The LORD has done great things for us,
    and we are filled with joy.

PSALM 126:2-3

I will rejoice in the LORD,
    I will be joyful in God my Savior.

HABAKKUK 3:18

Surely God is my salvation;
    I will trust and not be afraid.
The LORD, the LORD, is my strength and my
        song;
    he has become my salvation.
With joy you will draw water
    from the wells of salvation.
In that day you will say:
    "Give thanks to the LORD, call on his name;
    make known among the nations what he has
        done,
    and proclaim that his name is exalted.
Sing to the LORD, for he has done glorious things;
    let this be known to all the world."

ISAIAH 12:2–5

LONELINESS

God has said,
"Never will I leave you;
never will I forsake you."

HEBREWS 13:5

Abide with me! Fast falls the even-tide;
The darkness deepens: Lord, with me abide!
When other helpers fail, and comforts flee,
Help of the helpless, O abide with me!

I need Thy presence every passing hour—
What but Thy grace can foil the tempter's power?
Who like Thyself my guide and stay can be?
Thru cloud and sunshine, O abide with me!

I fear no foe with Thee at hand to bless,
Ills have no weight and tears no bitterness;
Where is death's sting? Where, grave, thy victory?
I triumph still if Thou abide with me!

JOHN KEBLE

Jesus said, "I will not leave you as orphans;
I will come to you."

JOHN 14:18

I am poor and needy;
*   may the Lord think of me.*
You are my help and my deliverer;
*   O my God, do not delay.*

PSALM 40:17

"I will be a Father to you,
and you will be my sons and daughters,
says the Lord Almighty."

2 CORINTHIANS 6:18

The LORD said, "I am with you and will watch
over you wherever you go . . . . I will not leave
you until I have done what I have promised you."

GENESIS 28:15

You will call, and the Lord will answer;
*   you will cry for help, and he will say:*
*   Here am I.*

ISAIAH 58:9

You are a chosen people, a royal priesthood, a holy nation, a people belonging to God, that you may declare the praises of him who called you out of darkness into his wonderful light.

1 PETER 2:9

Jesus said, "I will ask the Father, and he will give you another Counselor to be with you forever—the Spirit of truth. The world cannot accept him, because it neither sees him nor knows him. But you know him, for he lives with you and will be in you."

JOHN 14:16–17

Jesus said, "If anyone loves me, he will obey my teaching. My Father will love him, and we will come to him and make our home with him."

JOHN 14:23

You are a people holy to the Lord your God. The Lord your God has chosen you out of all the peoples on the face of the earth to be his people, his treasured possession.

DEUTERONOMY 7:6

The Lord stood at my side and gave me strength.

2 TIMOTHY 4:17

Turn to me and be gracious to me, LORD,
    for I am lonely and afflicted.
The troubles of my heart have multiplied;
    free me from my anguish.
Look upon my affliction and my distress
    and take away all my sins.
See how my enemies have increased
    and how fiercely they hate me!
Guard my life and rescue me;
    let me not be put to shame,
    for I take refuge in you.

PSALM 25:16–20

If anyone acknowledges that Jesus is the Son of
God, God lives in him and he in God. And so we
know and rely on the love God has for us.

1 JOHN 4:15–16

A father to the fatherless, a defender of widows,
    is God in his holy dwelling.
God sets the lonely in families,
    he leads forth the prisoners with singing.

PSALM 68:5–6

Find rest, O my soul, in God alone;
    my hope comes from him.

PSALM 62:5

Answer me quickly, O LORD;
    my spirit fails.
Do not hide your face from me
    or I will be like those who go down to the pit.
Let the morning bring me word of your
        unfailing love,
    for I have put my trust in you.
Show me the way I should go,
    for to you I lift up my soul.

PSALM 143:7-8

Grant me, gracious Lord,
    a pure intention of my heart,
    and a steadfast regard to thy glory
        in all my actions.
Possess my mind continually with thy presence,
and ravish it with thy love, that my only delight
    may be, to be embraced in the
        arms of thy protection.

JOHN COSIN

PATIENCE

Be patient, . . .
until the Lord's coming. See how the farmer
waits for the land to yield its valuable
crop and how patient he is for the
autumn and spring rains.
Be patient and stand firm,
because the Lord's coming is near.

JAMES 5:7–8

Fill us with enough patience, O Lord, to love one
another and share your goodness and graciousness
with others even when we don't feel like doing so.
Renew in use the gifts of the Spirit:

> *Increase our compassion and kindness to all*
> *mankind*
> *Make our words be gentle and humble*
> *And above all,*
> *Make us paiient as we wait for the future*
> *and for your conitnuing glory.*

> *Amen*

DORIS W. RIKKERS

Jesus said, "Since you have kept my command to endure patiently, I will also keep you from the hour of trial that is going to come upon the whole world to test those who live on the earth.

REVELATION 3:10

Live a life worthy of the calling you have received. Be completely humble and gentle; be patient, bearing with one another in love. Make every effort to keep the unity of the Spirit through the bond of peace

EPHESIANS 4:1–3

You, O Lord, are a compassionate and gracious God,
slow to anger, abounding in love
and faithfulness.

PSALM 86:15

Love is patient.

1 CORINTHIANS 13:4

There is a time for everything,
    and a season for every activity under heaven.

ECCLESIASTES 3:1

Be joyful in hope, patient in affliction,
faithful in prayer.

ROMANS 12:12

As God's chosen people, holy and dearly loved,
clothe yourselves with compassion, kindness,
humility, gentleness and patience

COLOSSIANS 3:12

A man's wisdom gives him patience;
    it is to his glory to overlook an offense.

PROVERBS 19:11

The end of a matter is better than its beginning,
and patience is better than pride.

ECCLESIASTES 7:8

The fruit of the Spirit is love, joy, peace, patience,
kindness, goodness, faithfulness, gentleness and
self-control. Against such things there is no law.

GALATIANS 5:22–23

I wait for the LORD, my soul waits,
    and in his word I put my hope.
My soul waits for the Lord
    more than watchmen wait for the morning,
    more than watchmen wait for the morning.

PSALM 130:5–6

Be still before the LORD and wait patiently for him;
    do not fret when men succeed in their ways,
    when they carry out their wicked schemes.

PSALM 37:7

LORD, walking in the way of your laws,
    we wait for you;
your name and renown
    are the desire of our hearts.

ISAIAH 26:8

If we hope for what we do not yet have,
we wait for it patiently.

ROMANS 8:25

Do not forget this one thing, dear friends:
With the Lord a day is like a thousand years,
and a thousand years are like a day. The Lord is
not slow in keeping his promise, as some
understand slowness. He is patient with you,
not wanting anyone to perish, but everyone to
come to repentance ... Bear in mind that our
Lord's patience means salvation.

2 PETER 3:8—9, 15

I waited patiently for the LORD;
*   he turned to me and heard my cry.*
He lifted me out of the slimy pit,
*   out of the mud and mire;*
he set my feet on a rock
*   and gave me a firm place to stand.*
He put a new song in my mouth,
*   a hymn of praise to our God.*
Many will see and fear
*   and put their trust in the LORD.*

PSALM 40:1—3

PEACE

Jesus said, "Peace I leave with you;
my peace I give you.
I do not give to you as the world gives.
Do not let your hearts be troubled
and do not be afraid."

JOHN 14:27

Grant Peace,
We Pray, in Mercy, Lord
Grant peace, we pray, in mercy, Lord;
Peace in our time, oh send us!
For there is none other on earth but you,
None other to defend us.
You only, Lord, can fight for us.
Amen

MARTIN LUTHER

God will judge between the nations
    and will settle disputes for many peoples.
They will beat their swords into plowshares
    and their spears into pruning hooks.
Nation will not take up swords against nation,
    nor will they train for war anymore.

ISAIAH 2:4

The mind of sinful man is death, but the mind
controlled by the Spirit is life and peace.

ROMANS 8:6

Aim for perfection. Listen to my appeal, be of
one mind, live in peace. And the God of love and
peace will be with you.

2 CORINTHIANS 13:11

I will lie down and sleep in peace,
    for you alone, O LORD,
    make me dwell in safety.

PSALM 4:8

May the Lord of peace himself give you peace
at all times and in every way.

2 THESSALONIANS 3:16

"I will grant peace in the land, and you will lie down and no one will make you afraid,"
says the LORD.

ISAIAH 26:6

The fruit of righteousness will be peace;
*   the effect of righteousness will be quietness*
*   and confidence forever.*

ISAIAH 32:17

I will listen to what God the LORD will say;
*   he promises peace to his people, his saints.*

PSALM 85:8

Lord, you establish peace for us;
*   all that we have accomplished you have*
*   done for us.*

ISAIAH 26:12

Great peace have they who love your law,
*   and nothing can make them stumble.*

PSALM 119:165

You will keep in perfect peace
*   him whose mind is steadfast,*
*   because he trusts in you.*

ISAIAH 26:3

The wisdom that comes from heaven is first of all pure; then peace-loving, considerate, submissive, full of mercy and good fruit, impartial and sincere. Peacemakers who sow in peace raise a harvest of righteousness.

JAMES 3:17–18

How beautiful on the mountains
*   are the feet of those who bring good news,*
who proclaim peace,
*   who bring good tidings,*
*   who proclaim salvation,*
who say to Zion,
*   "Your God reigns!"*

ISAIAH 52:7

Blessed are the peacemakers,
for they will be called sons of God.

MATTHEW 5:9

Lord,
we pray for the power to be gentle;
the strength to be forgiving;
the patience to be understanding;
and the endurance to accept the consequences of
holding to what we believe to be right.

Help us to devote our whole life and
thought and energy to the task of making peace,
praying always for the inspiration
and the power to fulfill the destiny for which
we and all men were created.

WEEK OF PRAYER FOR WORLD PEACE, 1978

PRAISE

Praise the Lord!
How good it is to sing praises to our God,
how pleasant and fitting
to praise him!

PSALM 147:1

We give praise and glory to you,
most blessed Trinity,
for the blessing of our creation, by which you
granted us bodies and souls,
you adorned us with your image and likeness,
and added us to your Christian flock,
making us sound and whole in our senses
and in our members,
above all the creatures who are beneath the heavens,
and gave us your holy angels
as our guides and ministers.
For all this be pleased that we may praise you,
world without end.

LATIN PRAYER

Clap your hands, all you nations;
    shout to God with cries of joy.
How awesome is the LORD Most High,
    the great King over all the earth!

PSALM 47:1–2

I will praise you with the harp
    for your faithfulness, O my God;
I will sing praise to you with the lyre,
    O Holy One of Israel.
My lips will shout for joy
    when I sing praise to you—
    I, whom you have redeemed.

PSALM 71:22–23

Let them praise his name with dancing
    and make music to him with tambourine
        and harp.
For the LORD takes delight in his people;
    he crowns the humble with salvation.

PSALM 149:3–4

Since we are receiving a kingdom that cannot be shaken, let us be thankful, and so worship God acceptably with reverence and awe.

HEBREWS 12:28

O LORD, our Lord,
   how majestic is your name in all the earth!
You have set your glory
   above the heavens.
From the lips of children and infants
   you have ordained praise.

PSALM 8:1–2

Whenever the living creatures give glory, honor
and thanks to God who sits on the throne and who
lives for ever and ever, the twenty-four elders fall
down before him who sits on the throne, and
worship him who lives for ever and ever. They lay
their crowns before the throne and say:
   "You are worthy, our Lord and God,
      to receive glory and honor and power,
   for you created all things,
      and by your will they were created
      and have their being."

REVELATION 4:9–11

Praise be to the God and Father of our Lord Jesus
Christ! In his great mercy he has given us new
birth into a living hope through the resurrection
of Jesus Christ from the dead.

1 PETER 1:3

PRAYER

*This is the confidence
we have in approaching God:
that if we ask anything according to his will,
he hears us.
And if we know that he hears us—
whatever we ask—
we know that we have what we asked of him.*

1 JOHN 5:14–15

May the words of my mouth and the meditation
of my heart
be pleasing in your sight,
O LORD, my Rock and my Redeemer.

PSALM 19:14

I called on your name, O LORD,
from the depths of the pit.
You heard my plea: "Do not close you ears
to my cry for relief."
You came near when I called you,
and you said, "Do not fear."

LAMENTATIONS 3:55–57

What other nation is so great as to have their gods
near them the way the LORD our God is near us
whenever we pray to him?

DEUTERONOMY 4:7

When you pray, go into your room, close the
door and pray to your Father, who is unseen.
Then your Father, who sees what is done in
secret, will reward you.

MATTHEW 6:6

In my distress I called to the LORD,
   and he answered me.

JONAH 2:2

O LORD, I call to you; come quickly to me.
   Hear my voice when I call to you.
May my prayer be set before you like incense;
   may the lifting up of my hands be like the
      evening sacrifice.

PSALM 141:1—2

The LORD has heard my cry for mercy;
   the LORD accepts my prayer.

PSALM 6:9

Jesus said, "Whatever you ask for in prayer,
believe that you have received it, and it will
be yours."

MARK 11:24

The prayer of a righteous man is
powerful and effective.

JAMES 5:16

Pray in the Spirit on all occasions with all kinds of prayers and requests. With this in mind, be alert and always keep on praying for all the saints.

EPHESIANS 6:18

I urge, then, first of all, that requests, prayers, intercession and thanksgiving be made for everyone—for kings and all those in authority, that we may live peaceful and quiet lives in all godliness and holiness.

1 TIMOTHY 2:1–2

The Spirit helps us in our weakness. We do not know what we ought to pray for, but the Spirit himself intercedes for us with groans that words cannot express.

ROMANS 8:26

This is what the LORD says, he who made the earth, the LORD who formed it and established it—the LORD is his name: "Call to me and I will answer you and tell you great and unsearchable things you do not know."

JEREMIAH 33:3

By day the LORD directs his love
at night his song is with me—
a prayer to the God of my life.

PSALM 42:8

The prayer offered in faith will make the sick
person well; the Lord will raise him up. If he has
sinned, he will be forgiven. Therefore confess
your sins to each other and pray for each other
so that you may be healed.

JAMES 5:15–16

Know that the LORD has set apart the
godly for himself;
the LORD will hear when I call to him.

PSALM 4:3

This is the confidence we have in approaching
God: that if we ask anything according to his will,
he hears us. And if we know that he hears us—
whatever we ask—we know that we have what
we asked of him.

1 JOHN 5:14–15

The righteous cry out, and the LORD hears them;
   he delivers them from all their troubles.

PSALM 34:17

Hear my prayer, O LORD;
   listen to my cry for mercy.
In the day of my trouble I will call to you
   for you will answer me.

PSALM 86:6−7

This, then, is how you should pray:
"Our Father in heaven,
hallowed be your name,
your kingdom come,
your will be done
   on earth as it is in heaven.
Give us today our daily bread.
Forgive us our debts,
   as we also have forgiven our debtors.
And lead us not into temptation,
but deliver us from the evil one."

MATTHEW 6:9−13

PRESENCE
of GOD

*God is not far from
each one of us.*

ACTS 17:27

Our Father and Almighty God,
Fill our hearts, our minds,
our actions and words with your presence.
Let your love fill our lives
so completely that your presence and peace
shine in and through us;
and as your servants,
we become a blessing to all whose lives we touch.
Amen

DORIS W. RIKKERS

Jesus said, "Where two or three come together in my name, there am I with them."

MATTHEW 18:20

Where can I go from your Spirit, O LORD?
    Where can I flee from your presence?
If I go up to the heavens, you are there;
    if I make my bed in the depths, you are there.
If I rise on the wings of the dawn,
    if I settle on the far side of the sea,
even there your hand will guide me,
    your right hand will hold me fast.

PSALM 139:7–10

If you seek the LORD, he will be found by you.

1 CHRONICLES 28:9

The LORD is with you when you are with him.

2 CHRONICLES 15:2

The virgin will be with child and will give birth
to a son, and they will call him Immanuel—
which means, "God with us."

MATTHEW 1:23

No one has ever seen God; but if we love one
another, God lives in us and his love is made
complete in us.

1 JOHN 4:12

You have made known to me the paths of life,
  O Lord;
 you will fill me with joy in your presence.

ACTS 2:28

From birth I was cast upon you;
 from my mother's womb you have been my God.
Do not be far from me,
 for trouble is near
 and there is no one to help.

PSALM 22:10–11

Come near to God and he will come near to you.

JAMES 4:8

And I heard a loud voice from the throne [of heaven] saying, "Now the dwelling of God is with men, and he will live with them. They will be his people, and God himself will be with them and be their God."

REVELATION 21:3

One thing I ask of the LORD,
    this is what I seek:
that I may dwell in the house of the LORD
    all the days of my life,
to gaze upon the beauty of the LORD
    and to seek him in his temple.

PSALM 27:4

This is what the LORD says ...
When you pass through the waters,
    I will be with you;
and when you pass through the rivers,
    they will not sweep over you.
When you walk through the fire,
    you will not be burned;
    the flames will not set you ablaze.

ISAIAH 43:1–2

You hem me in—behind and before;
    you have laid your hand upon me.
Such knowledge is too wonderful for me,
    too lofty for me to attain.
Where can I go from your Spirit?
Where can I flee from your presence?
If I go up to the heavens, you are there;
    if I make my bed in the depths, you are there.
If I rise on the wings of the dawn,
    if I settle on the far side of the sea,
    even there your hand will guide me,
    your right hand will hold me fast.

PSALM 139:5–10

In my integrity you uphold me
    and set me in your presence forever.
Praise be to the LORD, the God of Israel,
    from everlasting to everlasting.
    Amen

PSALM 41:12–13

PROTECTION

You are my hiding place;
you will protect me from trouble
and surround me with songs
of deliverance.

PSALM 32:7

O God our Father,
by whose mercy and might the world turns safely
into darkness and returns again to light:

We give into they hands our unfinished task,
our unsolved problems, and our unfulfilled hopes,
knowing that only that which thou dost bless
will prosper.

To thy great love and protection
we commit each other and all those we love knowing
that thou alone art our sure defender,
through Jesus Christ, our Lord.

THE CHURCH OF SOUTH INDIA

Let all who take refuge in you, be glad, O LORD;
     let them ever sing for joy.
Spread your protection over them,
     that those who love your name may rejoice in you.

PSALM 5:11

Be exalted, O God, above the heavens,
     and let your glory be over all the earth.
Save us and help us with your right hand,
     that those you love may be delivered.

PSALM 108:5–6

The eternal God is your refuge,
     and underneath are the everlasting arms.

DEUTERONOMY 33:27

Do not withhold your mercy from me, O LORD;
     may your love and your truth always protect me.

PSALM 40:11

The LORD is a refuge for the oppressed,
     a stronghold in times of trouble.

PSALM 9:9

The Lord holds victory in store for the upright,
    he is a shield to those whose walk is
        blameless,
for he guards the course of the just
    and protects the way of his faithful ones.

PROVERBS 2:7–8

O LORD, you will keep us safe
    and protect us ... forever.

PSALM 12:7

The LORD watches over you—
    the LORD is your shade at your right hand;
the sun will not harm you by day,
    nor the moon by night.
The LORD will keep you from all harm—
    he will watch over your life;
the LORD will watch over your coming and going
    both now and forevermore.

PSALM 121:5–8

Keep me as the apple of your eye;
    hide me in the shadow of your wings.

PSALM 17:8

STRENGTH

*It is God who arms me with strength
and makes my way perfect.*

2 SAMUEL 22:33

Lord God Almighty,
The Father of our Lord Jesus Christ,
You gave strength to your prophets
And your holy apostles,
You gave strength to your holy martyrs,
May you also give strength to us,
And protect us from harm.
Take our souls to yourself with our
faces unashamed.
To you be glory, and to your beloved
And holy Son Jesus Christ and the
Holy Spirit, forever and ever.
Amen

PAESE THE COPT

God is our refuge and strength,
     an ever-present help in trouble.
Therefore we will not fear, though the earth give way
     and the mountains fall into the heart of the sea.

PSALM 46:1–2

Look to the LORD and his strength;
     seek his face always.
Remember the wonders he has done,
     his miracles, and the judgments he
          pronounced.

1 CHRONICLES 16:11–12

The LORD gives strength to the weary
     and increases the power of the weak.
Even youths grow tired and weary,
     and young men stumble and fall;
but those who hope in the LORD
     will renew their strength.
They will soar on wings like eagles;
     they will run and not grow weary,
     they will walk and not be faint.

ISAIAH 40:29–31

Surely God is my salvation;
*   I will trust and not be afraid.*
The LORD, the LORD, is my strength and my song;
*   he has become my salvation.*

ISAIAH 12:2

The LORD is my strength and my shield;
*   my heart trusts in him, and I am helped.*
My heart leaps for joy
*   and I will give thanks to him in song.*

PSALM 28:7

You are awesome, O God...
*   the God of Israel gives power and strength*
to his people.

PSALM 68:35

Be strong in the Lord and in his mighty power.

EPHESIANS 6:10

The foolishness of God is wiser than man's
wisdom, and the weakness of God is stronger
than man's strength.

1 CORINTHIANS 1:25

The Sovereign LORD is my strength;
> *he makes my feet like the feet of a deer,*
> *he enables me to go on the heights.*

HABAKKUK 3:19

My flesh and my heart may fail,
> *but God is the strength of my heart*
> *and my portion forever.*

PSALM 73:26

I will sing of your strength, O God,
> *in the morning I will sing of your love;*
for you are my fortress,
> *my refuge in times of trouble.*

PSALM 59:16

I pray that the eyes of your heart may be
enlightened in order that you may know. . .
his incomparably great power for us who believe.
That power is like the working of his mighty
strength, which he exerted in Christ when he
raised him from the dead and seated him at his
right hand in the heavenly realms.

EPHESIANS 1:18–20

"Do not fear, for I am with you;
    do not be dismayed, for I am your God.
I will strengthen you and help you;
    I will uphold you with my righteous right
        hand."

ISAIAH 41:10

One thing God has spoken,
    two things have I heard:
that you, O God, are strong,
    and that you, O LORD, are loving.

PSALM 62:11–12

O God,
I am so weak, and you are so strong.
I know that in your strength I can do anything.
Give me peace to face the choices of yesterday.
Give me strength to face the tasks of today.
Give me hope to face the challenges of tomorrow.
Amen.

DORIS W. RIKKERS

STRESS

The LORD Almighty says,
"I will refresh the weary and
satisfy the faint."

JEREMIAH 31:25

The Lord Jesus Christ be near
to defend thee,
within thee to refresh thee,
around thee to preserve thee,
before thee to guide thee,
behind thee to justify thee,
above thee to bless thee;
who liveth and reigneth with the father
and the Holy Spirit,
God for evermore.

ANONYMOUS

Answer me when I call to you,
O my righteous God.
Give me relief from my distress;
be merciful to me and hear my prayer.

PSALM 4:1

This is what the Sovereign LORD,
the Holy One of Israel says:
"In repentance and rest is your salvation,
in quietness and trust is your strength."

ISAIAH 30:15

The Lord is my shepherd, I shall not be in want.
    He makes me lie down in green pastures,
he leads me beside quiet waters,
    he restores my soul.

PSALM 23:1—3

In vain you rise early
    and stay up late,
toiling for food to eat—
    for God grants sleep to those he loves.

PSALM 127:2

Let the peace of Christ rule in your hearts, since
as members of one body you were called to
peace. And be thankful.

COLOSSIANS 3:15

Jesus said, "Come to me, all you who are weary
and burdened, and I will give you rest. Take my
yoke upon you and learn from me, for I am
gentle and humble in heart, and you will find
rest for your souls. For my yoke is easy and
my burden is light."

MATTHEW 11:28—30

There remains, then, a Sabbath-rest for the people of God; for anyone who enters God's rest also rests from his own work, just as God did from his. Let us, therefore, make every effort to enter that rest.

HEBREWS 4:9–11

And now, O God,
give me a quiet mind, as I lie down to rest.
Dwell in my thoughts until sleep overtakes me.
Let me not be fretted by any anxiety
over the lesser interests of life.
Let no troubled dreams disturb me,
so that I may awake refreshed and ready for
the tasks of another day.

JOHN BAILLIE

Trust

Trust in the LORD forever,
for the LORD, the LORD,
is the Rock eternal.

ISAIAH 26:4

Almighty God,
In you I trust, I will not be afraid.
I put all my trust in you
for you have been my help,
my comfort and my hope through
all the years of my life.
In times of difficulty, I have trusted you
and you have remained faithful to me.

I trust you now, O Lord.
Show me what I should do today
and the way that I should go that will bring
glory and honor to your name.
In Jesus' name I pray,
Amen

DORIS W. RIKKERS

When I am afraid,
I will trust in you.
In God, whose word I praise,
in God I trust; I will not be afraid.
What can mortal man do to me?

PSALM 56:3−4

Trust in the LORD with all your heart
and lean not on your own understanding;
in all your ways acknowledge him,
and he will make your paths straight.

PROVERBS 3:5−6

The LORD is good,
a refuge in times of trouble.
He cares for those who trust in him.

NAHUM 1:7

He who dwells in the shelter of the Most High
will rest in the shadow of the Almighty.
I will say of the LORD, "He is my refuge and
my fortress,
my God, in whom I trust."

PSALM 91:1−2

Let the morning bring me word of your
        unfailing love, O Lord,
    for I have put my trust in you.
Show me the way I should go,
    for to you I lift up my soul.

PSALM 143:8

Let him who walks in the dark,
    who has no light,
trust in the name of the LORD
    and rely on his God.

ISAIAH 50:10

Commit your way to the LORD;
    trust in him and he will do this:
He will make your righteousness shine like the dawn,
    the justice of your cause like the noonday sun.

PSALM 37:5–6

The LORD will guide you always;
    he will satisfy your needs in a sun-scorched
        land
    and will strengthen your frame.
You will be like a well-watered garden,
    like a spring whose waters never fail.

ISAIAH 58:11

WISDOM

*Know also that
wisdom is sweet to your soul;
if you find it,
there is a future hope for you,
and your hope will not be cut off.*

PROVERBS 24:14

Get wisdom, get understanding;
   do not forget my words or swerve from them.
Do not forsake wisdom, and she will protect you;
   love her, and she will watch over you.

PROVERBS 4:5–6

To the man who pleases him, God gives wisdom,
knowledge and happiness.

ECCLESIASTES 2:26

Those who are wise will shine like the brightness
of the heavens, and those who lead many to
righteousness, like the stars for ever and ever.

DANIEL 12:3

If any of you lacks wisdom, he should ask God,
who gives generously to all without finding fault,
and it will be given to him.

JAMES 1:5

The fear of the LORD is the beginning of wisdom,
   and knowledge of the Holy One is
      understanding.

PROVERBS 9:10

Who is wise and understanding among you? Let him show it by his good life, by deeds done in the humility that comes from wisdom.

JAMES 3:13

Wisdom, like an inheritance, is a good thing
and benefits those who see the sun.
Wisdom is a shelter
as money is a shelter,
but the advantage of knowledge is this:
that wisdom preserves the life of its possessor.

ECCLESIASTES 7:11–12

Almighty God,
from whom all thoughts of truth and peace proceed:
Kindle, we pray thee, in the hearts of all men
the true love of peace; and guide with thy pure and
peaceable wisdom those who take counsel for the
nations of the earth; that in tranquility thy
kingdom may go forward, till the earth is filled
with the knowledge of they love;
through Jesus Christ our Lord.

BISHOP FRANCIS PAGET

Also available from Inspirio:

Promises & Prayers for You in the Military
From the New International Version

At Inspirio we love to hear from you—
your stories, your feedback,
and your product ideas.
Please send your comments to us
by way of e-mail at
icares@zondervan.com
or to the address below:

inspirio

Attn: Inspirio Cares
5300 Patterson Avenue SE
Grand Rapids, MI 49530

If you would like further information
about Inspirio and the products we
create please visit us at:
www.inspiriogifts.com

Thank you and God Bless!